A MUSICAL HELL

EL INFIERNO MUSICAL

NEW DIRECTIONS POETRY PAMPHLETS

A MUSICAL HELL

EL INFIERNO MUSICAL

Alejandra Pizarnik

Preface by Julio Cortázar

Translated from the Spanish by Yvette Siegert

NEW DIRECTIONS POETRY PAMPHLET #6

Cover design by Office of Paul Sahre
Interior design by Eileen Baumgartner and Erik Rieselbach
Manufactured in the United States of America
New Directions Books are printed on acid-free paper.
First published as New Directions Poetry Pamphlet #6 in 2013
Published simultaneously in Canada by Penguin Books Canada Limited

Library of Congress Cataloging-in-Publication Data
Pizarnik, Alejandra, 1936–1972.
[Infierno musical. English]
A musical hell / Alejandra Pizarnik; translated from the Spanish by Yvette Siegert.
pages cm. — (A New Directions Poetry pamphlet; #6)
Includes bibliographical references.
ISBN 978-0-8112-2096-5 (alk. paper)
I. Title.
PQ7797.P5761513 2013
861'.64—dc23

2013005433

10 9 8 7 6 5 4 3 2 1

New Directions Books are published for James Laughlin
by New Directions Publishing Corporation
80 Eighth Avenue, New York 10011

CONTENTS

III. Figuras de la ausencia / The Shapes of Absence

IV. Los poseídos entre lilas / The Possessed among the Lilacs

PREFACE

From a Letter to Alejandra Pizarnik from Julio Cortázar

Alejandrísima,

Your secret popularity inhabits the balconies of the Latin Quarter. There's a painter here who signs his work *Piza*; another signs his *Arnik*. Someone's come out with a cocktail called the Alejandra. And a notorious plagiarist named Hesiod has published a book called *Works and Days*.

It's tough not to be an idiot in a letter, when one is what one is and nothing else. Years ago it hit me that I could turn a letter into a kind of book review for the author's private use. Possibly everything that your book does to me can best be described with looseleaf words or with drawings. I'm no good at drawings, but words—sure—so:

cockroach
      mandrake
           lantern
              unicorn
                closet moths
                    hole (so full, so full)

Your book hurts me. It's utterly your own; you're so *you* in every line, so reticently clear. You are underneath it and inside of it. You've heard of this reviewing method where you page through a book and cite various verses and passages, then make some comment to praise or shoot it down? I don't care for this sort of thing. But I'm going to say to you that what the book makes me feel is the same thing I feel standing in front of certain (very few) paintings or drawings by the Surrealists: that for a second I'm on the other side, that they have helped me cross over, that I'm *you*, that I'm dangling from the end of the thread like one of those red spiders you see in Provence that seem to have formed an alliance with Darkness. Now I know that everything, or almost everything, can be said in very few words. Each of your poems is the cube of an enormous wheel. Other people fashion a complete wheel, and then you have to figure out how it got stuck in the ditch; you, on the other hand, let the wheel turn into something else, something that a select few can see being drawn outside the page. And so Ben-Hur's chariot wins the race with its airborne wheels, while the ones fitted with oak or bronze wheels are left in the dust. Your poems are like tiny engravings, or better yet, like Babylonian cylinders, and one of these days I will take you to the Louvre and show you one of these cylinders I discovered there recently, in the Etruscan room. The thing is probably not even Etruscan, since the Etruscans, for one thing, never made cylinders, they were so fucking backwards. But the conservative (or else radical) curator at the Louvre placed it in that room because he's a total cronopio, or maybe it's just there because there was no space left in the room for the Babylonian cylinders. In any case, I'll show it to you and it will make you jump up and down.

I fear that when it comes to your book, though, there are few who will be chosen. Only a few people will have lived in the necessary dimension to appreciate how so much can be contained in such (apparently) slight verbal correlatives. It's not that I have anything against long verse, it's just that there is something miraculous about a great brief poem. . . .

Fondly,
Julio

I. FIGURAS DEL PRESENTIMIENTO

I. THE SHAPES OF A PREMONITION

COLD IN HAND BLUES

y qué es lo que vas a decir
voy a decir solamente algo
y qué es lo que vas a hacer
voy a ocultarme en el lenguaje
y por qué
tengo miedo

COLD IN HAND BLUES

and what is it you're going to say
i'm just going to say something
and what's this you're going to do
i'm going to hide behind language
why
i'm afraid

PIEDRA FUNDAMENTAL

No puedo hablar con mi voz sino con mis voces.

Sus ojos eran la entrada del templo, para mí, que soy errante, que amo y muero. Y hubiese cantado hasta hacerme una con la noche, hasta deshacerme desnuda en la entrada del tiempo.

Un canto qu atravieso como un túnel.

Presencias inquietantes,
  gestos de figuras que se aparecen vivientes por obra de un lenguaje activo que las alude,
  signos que insinúan terrores insolubles.

Una vibración de los cimientos, un trepidar de los fundamentos, drenan y barrenan,
  y he sabido dónde se aposenta aquello tan otro que es yo, que espera que me calle para tomar posesión de mí y drenar y barrenar los cimientos, los fundamentos,
  aquello que me es adverso desde mí, conspira, toma posesión de mi terreno baldío,

  no,
    he de hacer algo,
  no,
    he de hacer nada,

  algo en mí no se abandona a la cascada de cenizas que me arrasa dentro de mí con ella que es yo, conmigo que soy ella y que soy yo, indeciblemente distinta de ella.

CORNERSTONE

I cannot speak with my voice, so I speak with my voices.

Those eyes were the entrance to the temple, for me, a wanderer who loves and dies—I would've sung until merging with the night, until dissolving naked at the beginning of time.

A song—a tunnel I pass through.

Disquieting presences,
gestures of figures that spring to life through the workings of
an active language that alludes to their shape,
signs insinuating insoluble terrors.

A trembling of the frame, a tremor through the foundation, the draining and drilling,
and I know where that thing is lodged—that great otherness of my self, that lies in wait for me to be silenced before it can take possession of me, and drain and drill into the frame, the foundation—
that part of my self that opposes from within, that schemes—
that takes possession of my fallowness,

no,
I should do something;
no,
I should do nothing at all;

something inside me won't give in to the avalanche of ash that can sweep through my insides with her who is me, with myself who is she and is I, unspeakably different from her.

En el silencio mismo (no en el mismo silencio) tragar noche, una noche inmensa inmersa en el sigilo de los pasos perdidos.

No puedo hablar para nada decir. Por eso nos perdemos, yo y el poema, en la tentativa inútil de transcribir relaciones ardientes.

¿A dónde la conduce esta escritura? A lo negro, a lo estéril, a lo fragmentado.

Las muñecas desventradas por mis antiguas manos de muñeca, la desilución al encontrar pura estopa (pura estepa tu memoria): el padre, que tuvo que ser Tiresias, flota en el río. Pero tú, ¿por qué te dejaste asesinar escuchando cuentos de álamos nevados?

Yo quería que mis dedos de muñeca penetraran en las teclas. Yo no quería rozar, como una araña, el teclado. Yo quería hundirme, clavarme, fijarme, petrificarme. Yo quería entrar en el teclado para entrar adentro de la música para tener una patria. Pero la música se movía, se apresuraba. Sólo cuando un refrán reincidía, alentaba en mí la esperanza de que se estableciera algo parecido a una estación de trenes, quiero decir: un punto de partida firme, desde el lugar, hacia el lugar, en unión y fusión con el lugar. Pero el refrán era demasiado breve, de modo que yo no podía fundar una estación pues no contaba más que con un tren algo salido de los rieles que se contorsionaba y se distorcionaba. Entonces abandoné la música y sus traiciones porque la música estaba más arriba o más abajo, pero no en el centro, en el lugar de la fusión y del encuentro. (Tú que fuiste mi única patria, ¿en dónde buscarte? Tal vez en este poema que voy escribiendo.)

To swallow the night in its very silence (which is not to say every silence)—a night that's immense, and immersed in the stealth of lost footsteps.

I can't just speak and say nothing. That's how we lose ourselves, the poem and I, in the hopeless attempt to write the things that burn.

Where does this writing lead her? To blackness, to the sterile and the fragmented.

Dolls gutted by my worn doll hands—the disappointment that they're made of burlap (and your memory, a barren lap): the priest—it must be Tiresias—is floating down the river. But as for you, why did you let them kill you while listening to that story of the snow-covered poplars?

I wanted my doll fingers to go inside the keys. I didn't want to pass lightly over the keyboard like a spider. What I wanted was to sink into it, to fasten and nail myself there, then harden into stone. I wanted to go into the keyboard in order to go inside the music and find my own country. But the music—it swayed, it rushed. Only in the refrains did it have any potential, because there I could hope that a structure resembling a train station might be built: a firm and steady starting point, a place for departures, for moving from the place, and to the place, and for being in union and fusion with the place. But the refrains were always too brief: I could never begin laying down a foundation, since I couldn't rely on there ever being more than one train—a slightly derailed one, at that, that contorted and contracted its spine. So I abandoned music and its treachery, because the music was either too high or too low, never at the center, in the place of fusion and encounter. (You who were my only country: where should I look for you? Maybe in this poem as I write it.)

Una noche en el circo recobré un lenguaje perdido en el momento que los jinetes con antorchas en la mano galopaban en ronda feroz sobre corceles negros. Ni en mis sueños de dicha existirá un coro de ángeles que suministre algo semejante a los sonidos calientes para mi corazón de los cascos contra las arenas.

(Y me dijo: Escribe; porque estas palabras son fieles y verdaderas.)

(Es un hombre o una piedra o un árbol el que va a comenzar el canto . . .)

Y era un estremecimiento suavemente trepidante (lo digo para aleccionar a la que extravió en mí su musicalidad y trepida con más disonancia que un caballo azuzado por una antorcha en las arenas de un país extranjero.)

Estaba abrazada al suelo diciendo un nombre. Creí que me había muerto y que la muerte era decir un nombre sin cesar.

No es esto, tal vez, lo que quiero decir. Este decir y decirse no es grato. No puedo hablar con mi voz sino con mis voces. También este poema es posible que sea una trampa, un escenario más.

Cuando el barco alternó su ritmo y vaciló en el agua violenta, me erguí como la amazona que domina solamente con sus ojos azules al caballo que se encabrita (¿o fue con sus ojos azules?). El agua verde en mi cara, he de beber de ti hasta que la noche se abra. Nadie puede salvarme pues soy invisible aun para mí que me llamo con tu voz. ¿En dónde estoy? Estoy en un jardín.

Hay un jardín.

One night, at the circus, I recovered a lost language—the very moment the horsemen furiously rode by with brandished torches on their black, galloping steeds. Not even in my wildest dreams could the angelic orders ever rally heartbeats to rival the hot, roiling sounds of those hooves across the desert.

(And he said unto me: Write, for these words are faithful and true.)

(A man or a stone or a tree will begin the song.)

It was a soft shudder. (Let this be a lesson for the one who lost her musicality in me and is shaking more dissonantly than a horse spooked by torches in a foreign country.)

I was cleaving to the floor, calling out a name. I thought I had died and that death meant repeating a name forever.

Maybe this isn't what I wanted to say. To speak, and speak of the self like this, is hardly easy. I cannot speak with my voice, so I speak with my voices. Or it could be that this poem is a trap, or simply another scene in a play.

When the ship lost its rhythm and began rocking on the violent water, I stood up like the Amazon who could subdue a rearing horse with just her blue eyes. (Or was it her blue eyes?) Greenish water on my face: I will drink from you until the night opens. No one can save me. I'm invisible even to myself. Here I am, calling to myself with your voice. Where am I? I am in a garden.

There is a garden.

OJOS PRIMITIVOS

En donde el miedo no cuenta cuentos y poemas, no forma figuras de terror y de gloria.

Vacío gris es mi nombre, mi pronombre.

Conozco la gama de los miedos y ese comenzar a cantar despacito en el desfiladero que reconduce hacia mi desconocida que soy, mi emigrante de sí.

Escribo contra el miedo. Contra el viento con garras que se aloja en mi respiración.

Y cuando por la mañana temes encontrarte muerta (y que no haya más imágenes): el silencio de la compresión, el silencio del mero estar, en esto se van los años, en estos se fue la bella alegría animal.

PRIMITIVE EYES

Where fear neither speaks in stories or poems, nor gives shape to terrors or triumphs.

My name, my pronoun—a grey void.

I'm familiar with the full range of fear. I know what it's like to start singing and to set off slowly through the narrow mountain pass that leads back to the foreigner in me, to my own expatriate.

I write to ward off fear and the clawing wind that lodges in my throat.

And in the morning, when you are afraid of finding yourself dead (of there being no more images): the silence of compression, the silence of existence itself. This is how the years fly by. This is how we lost that beautiful animal happiness.

EL INFIERNO MUSICAL

Golpean con soles

Nada se acopla con nada aquí

Y de tanto animal muerto en el cementerio de huesos filosos de mi memoria

Y de tantas monjas como cuervos que se precipitan a hurgar entre mis piernas

La cantidad de fragmentos me desgarra

Impuro diálogo

Un proyectarse desesperado de la materia verbal

Liberada a sí misma

Naufragando en sí misma

A MUSICAL HELL

They strike with suns

Nothing couples with anything here

And with so much carrion in this graveyard for the sharp bones of
my memory

And with so many nuns who rush like crows to poke between my legs

All these fragments rend me

Impure dialogue

A desperate expulsion of verbal matter

Free unto herself

Shipwrecking into herself

[handwritten annotation:] trans letron consists in rendering the impossible spin in guts

EL DESEO DE LA PALABRA

La noche, de nuevo la noche, la magistral sapiencia de lo oscuro, el cálido roce de la muerte, un instante de éxtasis para mí, heredera de todo jardín prohibido.

Pasos y voces del lado sombrío del jardín. Risas en el interior de las paredes. No vayas a creer que están vivos. No vayas a creer que no están vivos. En cualquier momento la fisura en la pared y el súbito desbandarse de las niñas que fui.

Caen niñas de papel de variados colores. ¿Hablan los colores? ¿Hablan las imágenes de papel? Solamente hablan las doradas y de ésas no hay ninguna por aquí.

Voy entre muros que se acercan, que se juntan. Toda la noche hasta la aurora salmodiaba: *Si no vino es porque no vino.* Pregunto. ¿A quién? Dice que pregunta, quiere saber a quién pregunta. Tú ya no hablas con nadie. Extranjera a muerte está muriéndose. Otro es el lenguaje de los agonizantes.

He malgastado el don de transfigurar a los prohibidos (los siento respirar adentro de las paredes). Imposible narrar mi día, mi vía. Pero contempla absolutamente sola la desnudez de estos muros. Ninguna flor crece ni crecerá del milagro. A pan y agua toda la vida.

DESIRE FOR THE WORD

Night, the night again, the magisterial wisdom of the dark. The warm brush of death—a moment of ecstasy for me, heir to every forbidden garden.

Footsteps and voices from the shadowy corners of the garden. Laughter inside the walls. Don't believe they're alive. Don't believe they're not alive. At any moment, the crack in the wall, the abrupt departure from the little girls I used to be.

Little paper girls of various colors are falling from the sky. Can colors speak? Can paper images speak? Only the gold ones speak, but there are no more of those around here.

I walk through sloping walls, walls that conjoin. From dusk till daybreak, chanting, *If someone didn't show up, it's because they didn't.* I ask. Whom? She claims to ask, she wants to know whom she is asking. You don't speak with anyone anymore. A stranger to death, she is dying. Those who attend to the dying have their own language for prayer.

I have wasted my gift for transfiguring exiles. (I can feel their breathing inside the walls.) Impossible to describe my days or my ways. But in her absolute solitude, she considers the nakedness of these high walls. There are no flowers there, and not even a miracle could make them grow. On a diet of bread and water for life.

En la cima de la alegría he declarado acerca de una música jamás oída. ¿Y qué? Ojalá pudiera vivir solamente en éxtasis, haciendo el cuerpo del poema con mi cuerpo, recatando cada frase con mis días y con mis semanas, infundiéndole al poema mi soplo a medida que cada letra de cada palabra haya sido sacrificada en las ceremonias del vivir.

At the height of happiness, I have spoken of a music never heard before. So what? If only I could live in a continual state of ecstasy, shaping the body of the poem with my own, rescuing every phrase with my days and weeks, imbuing the poem with my breath while feeding the letters of its every word into the offering in this ceremony of living.

LA PALABRA DEL DESEO

Esta espectral textura de la oscuridad, esta melodía en los huesos, este soplo de silencios diversos, este ir abajo por abajo, esta galería oscura, oscura, este hundirse sin hundirse.

¿Qué estoy diciendo? Está oscuro y quiero entrar. No sé qué más decir. (Yo no quiero decir, yo quiero entrar.) El dolor en los huesos, el lenguaje roto a paladas, poco a poco reconstituir el diagrama de la irrealidad.

Posesiones no tengo (esto es seguro: al fin algo seguro). Luego una melodía. Es una melodía plañidera, una luz lila, una inminencia sin destinatario. Veo la melodía. Presencia de una luz anaranjada. Sin tu mirada no voy a saber vivir, también esto es seguro. Te suscito, te resuscito. Y me dijo que saliera al viento y fuera de casa en casa preguntando si estaba.

Paso desnuda con un cirio en la mano, castillo frío, jardín de las delicias. La soledad no es estar parada en el muelle, a la madrugada, mirando el agua con avidez. La soledad es no poder decirla por no poder circundarla por no poder darle un rostro por no poder hacerla sinónima de un paisaje. La soledad sería esta melodía rota de mis frases.

THE WORD FOR DESIRE

This spectral texture of darkness, this melody in my bones, this breath from various silences, this going deeper and deeper, this dark, dark gallery, this sinking without sinking.

What am I saying? It's dark now and I want to go inside. I don't know what else to say. (And I don't want to say anything, I just want to go inside.) The ache in my bones. The language broken by spades—now reconstructing, bit by bit, a diagram of the unreal.

I have no possessions. (This is certain; at last, something certain.) Then a melody. It's a plaintive melody, a lilac light—imminence without a recipient. I see the melody, now the presence of an orange light. Without your eyes, I won't know how to live—this is also certain. I make you live, I revive you. And I was told to step out into the wind and knock on doors in search of them.

I walk past, naked, holding a taper. A cold castle, the garden of earthly delights. Solitude doesn't mean standing on a pier early in the morning, eagerly looking out over the water. Solitude is not being able to articulate the solitude, being unable to circumvent it, unable to give it a face, unable to make it a synonym for any landscape. Solitude would be this torn melody of my phrases.

NOMBRES Y FIGURAS

La hermosura de la infancia sombría, la tristeza imperdonable entre muñecas, estatuas, cosas mudas, favorables al doble monólogo entre yo y mi antro lujurioso, el tesoro de los piratas enterrado en mi primera persona del singular.

No se espera otra cosa que música y deja, deja que el sufrimiento que vibra en formas traidoras y demasiado bellas llegue al fondo de los fondos.

Hemos intentado hacernos perdonar lo que no hicimos, las ofensas fantásticas, las culpas fantasmas. Por bruma, por nadie, por sombras, hemos expiado.

Lo que quiero es honrar a la poseedora de mi sombra: la que sustrae de la nada nombres y figuras.

NAMES AND SHAPES

The beauty of my bleak childhood, the unforgivable sadness shared by dolls and statues—voiceless objects suitable for the double monologue between myself and the luxurious lair I live in, the pirate treasure buried in my first-person singular.

Waiting for nothing but music and allowing the pain—the pain that vibrates in forms too beautiful and treacherous—to reach down into the depths.

We've attempted to forgive ourselves for what we didn't do— the fantastic offenses, the phantom blaming. For the sea mist, for no one, for the shadows—for this we made amends.

What I want is honor the keeper of my shadow, the one who draws names and shapes out of nothing.

II. LAS UNIONES POSIBLES

II. POSSIBLE UNIONS

EN UN EJEMPLAR DE
LES CHANTS DE MALDOROR

Debajo de mi vestido ardía un campo con flores alegres como los niños de la medianoche.

El soplo de la luz en mis huesos cuando escribo la palabra tierra. Palabra o presencia seguida por animales perfumados; triste como sí misma, hermosa como el suicidio; y que me sobrevuela como una dinastía de soles.

SIGNOS

Todo hace el amor con el silencio.

Me habían prometido un silencio como un fuego, una casa de silencio.

De pronto el templo es un circo y la luz un tambor.

IN A COPY OF
LES CHANTS DE MALDOROR

Fields of flowers stung beneath my dress, giddy as children at midnight.

A gust of light in my bones when I write the word *earth*. A word or presence, followed by perfumed animals—as sad as itself, as beautiful as suicide—and it soars over me like a dynasty of suns.

SIGNS

Everything is making love to the silence.

They had promised me a silence like fire—a house of silence.

Suddenly, the temple is a circus and the light is a drum.

FUGA EN LILA

Había que escribir sin para qué, sin para quién.

El cuerpo se acuerda de un amor como encender la lámpara.

Si silencio es tentación y promesa.

DEL OTRO LADO

Como reloj de arena cae la música en la música.

Estoy triste en la noche de colmillos de lobo.

Cae la música en la música como mi voz en mis voces.

FUGUE IN LILAC

You had to write without a for what, without a for whom.

The body remembers love like the lighting of a lamp.

If silence is temptation and promise.

FROM THE OTHER SIDE

Like sand sifting through an hourglass, so music falls into music.

I am sad on this night made of wolf fangs.

Music falls into music the way my voice falls into my voices.

LAZO MORTAL

Palabras emitidas por un pensamiento a modo de tabla del náufrago. Hacer el amor adentro de nuestro abrazo significó una luz negra: la oscuridad se puso a brillar. Era la luz reencontrada, doblemente apagada pero de algún modo más viva que mil soles. El color del mausoleo infantil, el mortuario color de los detenidos deseos se abrió en la salvaje habitación. El ritmo de los cuerpos ocultaba el vuelo de los cuervos. El ritmo de los cuerpos cavaba un espacio de luz adentro de la luz.

MORTAL TIES

A single thought cast out words like lifelines at sea. Making love inside our embrace implied a black light: a darkness that started gleaming. A rediscovered light, twice extinguished already, yet more vibrant than a thousand suns. That savage room was made up in the deadened hues of repressed desire; its light was the color of a mausoleum for infants. The rhythm of our bodies disguised the flight of the ravens. The rhythm of our bodies carved out a space of light inside that light.

III. FIGURAS DE LA AUSENCIA

III. THE SHAPES OF ABSENCE

LA PALABRA QUE SANA

Esperando que un mundo sea desenterrado por el lenguaje, alguien canta el lugar en que se forma el silencio. Luego comprobará que no porque se muestre furioso existe el mar, ni tampoco el mundo. Por eso cada palabra dice lo que dice y además más y otra cosa.

LOS DE LO OCULTO

Para que las palabras no basten es preciso alguna muerte en el corazón.

La luz del lenguaje me cubre como una música, imagen mordida por los perros del desconsuelo, y el invierno sube por mí como la enamorada del muro.

Cuando espero dejar de esperar, sucede tu caída dentro de mí. Ya no soy más que un adentro.

THE WORD THAT HEALS

While waiting for a world to be unearthed by language, someone is singing about the place where silence is formed. Later it'll be shown that the display of fury is not what makes the sea—or the world—exist. In the same way, each word says what it says—and beyond that, something more and something else.

OF THINGS UNSEEN

Before words can run out, something in the heart must die.

The light of language covers me like music, like a picture ripped to shreds by the dogs of grief. And winter reaches for me like a woman who has fallen in love with a wall.

Just when I'd hoped to give up hoping, your fall takes place within me. No longer am I any more than this within.

L'OBSCURITÉ DES EAUX

Escucho resonar el agua que cae en mi sueño. Las palabras caen como el agua yo caigo. Dibujo en mis ojos la forma de mis ojos, nado en mis aguas, me digo mis silencios. Toda la noche espero que mi lenguaje logre configurarme. Y pienso en el viento que viene a mí, permanece en mí. Toda la noche he caminado bajo la lluvia desconocida. A mí me han dado un silencio pleno de formas y visiones (dices). Y corres desolada como el único pájaro en el viento.

GESTO PARA UN OBJETO

En tiempo dormido, un tiempo como un guante sobre un tambor.

Los tres que en mí contienden nos hemos quedado en el móvil punto fijo y no somos un es ni un estoy.

Antiguamente mis ojos buscaron refugio en las cosas humilladas, desamparadas, pero en amistad con mis ojos he visto, he visto y no aprobé.

L'OBSCURITÉ DES EAUX

Listening to the sounds of falling water in my dream. The words fall like the water—I fall. Drawing the shape of my eyes in my eyes; swimming in my waters and telling myself of my silences. All night long, waiting for language to configure me, I am thinking of the wind that whirls toward me and stays in me. All night long, I have been walking in an anonymous rain. I was given a silence filled with shapes and apparitions (you say). And you keep running, as unconsoled as a bird alone in the wind.

GESTURE FOR AN OBJECT

Numb time, time like a glove upon a drum.

The three who compete in me remain on a shifting point and we neither are nor is.

My eyes used to find rest in humiliated, forsaken things. Nowadays I see with them; I've seen and approved of nothing.

LA MÁSCARA Y EL POEMA

El espléndido palacio de papel de los peregrinajes infantiles.

A la puesta del sol pondrán a la volatinera en una jaula, la llevarán a un templo ruinoso y la dejarán allí sola.

ENDECHAS

I.

El lenguaje silencioso engendra fuego. El silencio se propaga, el silencio es fuego.

Era preciso decir acerca del agua o simplemente apenas nombrarla, de modo de atraerse la palabra agua para que apague las llamas de silencio.

Porque no cantó, su sombra canta. Donde una vez sus ojos hechizaron mi infancia, el silencio al rojo rueda como un sol.

En el corazón de la palabra lo alcanzaron; y yo no puedo narrar el espacio ausente y azul creado por sus ojos.

THE MASK AND THE POEM

The splendid paper palace of the wanderings of childhood.

When the sun sets, they will lock up the tightrope-walker in a cage and take her to the temple ruins and leave her there.

DIRGES

I.

Silent language breeds fire. Silence multiplies, silence is fire.

You had to speak of water—or simply name it—so as to coax the word *water* into extinguishing the blaze of silence.

Since it would not sing, its shadow sings. Once its eyes bewitched my childhood; now the red silence rolls away like a sun.

They caught up with it in the heart of the word, and it's impossible to describe the space—absent, blue—left by its eyes.

II.

Con una esponja húmeda de lluvia gris borraron el ramo de lilas dibujado en su cerebro.

El signo de su estar es la enlutada escritura de los mensajes que se envía. Ella se prueba en su nuevo lenguaje e indaga el peso del muerto en la balanza de su corazón.

III.

Y el signo de su estar crea el corazón de la noche.

Aprisionada: alguna vez se olvidarán las culpas, se emparentarán los vivos y los muertos.

Aprisionada: no has sabido prever que su final iría a ser la gruta a donde iban los malos en los cuentos para niños.

Aprisionada: deja que se cante como se pueda y se quiera. Hasta que en la merecida noche si cierna la brusca desocultada. A exceso de sufrimiento exceso de noche y de silencio.

IV.

Las metáforas de asfixia se despojan del sudario, el poema. El terror es nombrado con el modelo delante, a fin de no equivocarse.

V.

Y yo sola con mis voces, y tú, tanto estás del otro lado que te confundo conmigo.

II.

With a rain-grey sponge, they erased the sprigs of lilac etched onto her brain.

The sign of her existence is the mournful writing in the messages she sends to herself. She tests herself in her new language and weighs the man's corpse on the scale of her heart.

III.

And the sign of her existence shapes the heart of the night.

Prisoner, someday all faults will be forgotten. The living will form kinships with the dead.

Prisoner, there was no way to foresee that she would end up in the lair where all the villains go in fairytales.

Prisoner, sing this in any way you can, and any way you want. Until the appointed night when the woman will loom up abruptly, unveiled. For an excess of suffering, an excess of night, of silence.

IV.

Metaphors of suffocation unbind the poem—their shroud. Terror is identified with its model before it as a way of preventing error.

V.

And I, alone with my voices—and you, so far on the other side that I confuse you with myself.

A PLENA PÉRDIDA

Los sortilegios emanan del nuevo centro de un poema a nadie dirigido. Hablo con la voz que está detrás de la voz y emito los mágicos sonidos de la endechadora. Una mirada azul aureolaba mi poema. Vida, mi vida, ¿qué has hecho de mi vida?

TOTAL LOSS

Bits of sorcery emanate from the new core of a poem that isn't meant for anyone. I speak with a voice that lies beyond the voice and let out the potent cries of a mourner for hire. A blue glance has cast a halo around my poem. O life, what have you done to this life of mine?

IV. LOS POSEÍDOS ENTRE LILAS

IV. THE POSSESSED AMONG THE LILACS

I.

—Se abrió la flor de la distancia. Quiero que mires por la ventana y me digas lo que veas, gestos inconclusos, objetos ilusorios, formas fracasadas... Como si te hubieses preparado desde la infancia, acércate a la ventana.

—Un café lleno de sillas vacías, iluminado hasta la exasperación, la noche en forma de ausencia, el cielo como de una materia deteriorada, gotas de agua en una ventana, pasa alguien que no vi nunca, que no veré jamás...

—¿Qué hice del don de la mirada?

—Una lámpara demasiado intensa, una puerta abierta, alguien fuma en la sombra, el tronco y el follaje de un árbol, un perro se arrastra, una pareja de enamorados se pasea despacio bajo la lluvia, un diario en una zanja, un niño silbando...

—Proseguí.

—(En tono vengativo). Una equilibrista enana se echa al hombro una bolsa de huesos y avanza por el alambre con los ojos cerrados.

—¡No!

—Está desnuda pero lleva sombrero, tiene pelos por todas partes y es de color gris de modo que con sus cabellos rojos parece la chimenea de la escenografía teatral de un teatro para locos. Un gnomo desdentado la persigue mascando las lentejuelas...

—Basta, por favor.

I.

—The flower of distance is blooming. I want you to look through the window and tell me what you see: inconclusive gestures, illusory objects, failed shapes ... Go to the window as if you'd been preparing for this your entire life.

—A café filled with empty chairs—garishly lit ... The night takes on the shape of absence, and the sky of decay ... Drops of water on a windowpane—there goes someone I've never seen before and whom I'll never see again ...

—What did I ever do with the gift of sight?

—A lamp that's far too bright, an open door, someone smoking in the shadows, the trunk and leaves of a tree, a dog dragging its hind-legs, lovers lingering in the rain, a newspaper floating in a gully, a boy whistling ...

—Go on.

—(*Vengefully.*) A dwarf tightrope-walker heaves a sack of bones onto her shoulder and proceeds along the wire with her eyes shut.

—Oh, stop!

—She's naked but for her hat. She's hairy everywhere—and she's all grey, with a shock of red hair, so that the total effect makes her look like a fake chimney, like a stage prop in some play for the insane. A toothless gnome is chasing after her, munching on costume sequins ...

—Please, that's enough.

—(*En tono fatigado*). Una mujer grita, un niño llora. Siluetas espían desde sus madriagueras. Ha pasado un transeúnte. Se ha cerrado una puerta.

II.

Si viera un perro muerto me moriría de orfandad pensando en las caricias que recibió. Los perros son como la muerte: quieren huesos. Los perros comen huesos. En cuanto a la muerte, sin duda se entretiene tallándolos en forma de lapiceras, de cucharitas, de cortapapeles, de tenedores, de ceniceros. Sí, la muerte talla huesos en tanto el silencio es de oro y la palabra de plata. Sí, lo malo de la vida es que no es lo que creemos pero tampoco lo contrario.

Restos. Para nosotros quedan los huesos de los animales y de los hombres. Donde una vez un muchacho y una chica hacían el amor, hay cenizas y manchas de sangre y pedacitos de uñas y rizos púbicos y una vela doblegada que usaron con fines oscuros y manchas de esperma sobre el lodo y cabezas de gallos y una casa derruida dibujada en la arena y trozos de papeles perfumados que fueron cartas de amor y la rota bola de vidrio de una vidente y lilas marchitas y cabezas cortadas sobre almohadas como almas impotentes entre los asfódelos y tablas resquebrajadas y zapatos viejos y vestidos en el fango y gatos enfermos y ojos incrustados en una mano que se desliza hacia el silencio y manos con sortijas y espuma negra que salpica a un espejo que nada refleja y una niña que durmiendo asfixia a su paloma preferida y pepitas de oro negro resonantes como gitanos de duelo tocando sus violines a orillas del mar Muerto y un corazón que late para engañar y una rosa que se abre para traicionar y un niño llorando frente a un cuervo que grazna, y la inspiradora se enmascara para ejecutar una melodía

—(*Wearily.*) A woman is screaming. There's a boy crying. Silhouettes are spying from their lairs. Someone walked by just now. A door shuts . . .

II.

If I saw a dead dog, I would die like an orphan, thinking about all the caresses it had received. Dogs are like death: they want bones. Dogs eat bones. As for death, no doubt it amuses itself by whittling them into various shapes, like pens, little spoons, paper-knives, forks, ashtrays. Yes, death carves bones as long as silence is golden and words are made of silver. Yes, the bitch about life is that it's not what we think it is, but it's also not the opposite of that.

Mortal remains. Animal and human bones are left behind for us. Where a young couple used to make love, there are ashes and bloodstains and chipped nails and pubic hair and a bent candle once used for obscure purposes and sperm stains in the caked mud and condoms and a shambled house drawn in the sand and scraps of scented paper that were once love letters and the shattered glass ball of a fortune teller and wilted lilacs and severed heads lying on a pillow like impotent souls among the asphodels and cracked tables and old shoes and dresses in the mire and sick cats and eyes encrusted in a hand that slips away toward silence and other hands weighed down with signet rings and black foam spraying a mirror that gives no reflection and a young girl who suffocates her favorite dove in her sleep and black gold nuggets as resonant as gypsies in mourning who play their fiddles by the Dead Sea and a heart that lives for deception and a rose that blooms for betrayal and a boy crying in front of a raven that caws in the fields, and the muse puts on her mask to execute an inscrutable melody under a rain and it

que nadie entiende bajo una lluvia que calma mi mal. Nadie nos oye, por eso emitimos ruegos, pero ¡mira! el gitano más jóven está decapitando con sus ojos de serrucho a la niña de la paloma.

III.

Voces, rumores, sombras, cantos de ahogados: no sé si son signos o una tortura. Alguien demora en el jardín el paso del tiempo. Y las criaturas del otoño abandonadas al silencio.

Yo estaba predestinada a nombrar las cosas con nombres esenciales. Yo ya no existo y lo sé; lo que no sé es qué vive en lugar mío. Pierdo la razón si hablo, pierdo los años si callo. Un viento arrasó con todo. Y no haber podido hablar por todos aquellos que olvidaron el canto.

IV.

Alguna vez, tal vez, encontraremos refugio en la realidad verdadera. Entretanto ¿puedo decir hasta qué punto estoy en contra?

Te hablo de la soledad mortal. Hay cólera en el destino porque se acerca, entre las arenas y la piedras, el lobo gris. ¿Y entonces? Porque romperá todas las puertas, porque sacará afuera a los muertos para que devoren a los vivos, para que sólo haya muertos y los vivos desaparezcan. No tengas miedo del lobo gris. Yo lo nombré para comprobar que existe y porque hay una voluptuosidad en el hecho de comprobar.

soothes my suffering. No one can hear us, so we keep pleading, but—look there: with his handsaw eyes, the youngest gypsy is decapitating that young girl with the dove.

III.

Voices, rumors, shadows, the songs of the drowned: I don't know if they're signs or a kind of torture. Someone in the garden is delaying the passing of time. Autumn creatures abandoned to silence.

I was predestined to give things their essential names. I know that I no longer exist, but what I don't know is the thing that lives on in my place. I lose my senses if I speak—I lose all wisdom if I keep quiet. A violent wind has wiped out everything. And not being able to speak for those who forgot how to sing.

IV.

Maybe someday we'll find refuge in true reality. In the meantime, can I just say how opposed I am to all of this?

I'm speaking to you of a mortal solitude. Destiny is red with rage because the grey wolf who lurks between the sand and the rocks is drawing nearer. Then what? Because it will knock down every door, and unearth the dead and have them devour the living, so that only the dead remain and all the living disappear. But don't be afraid of the grey wolf. I named it in order to confirm that it exists, and because the very act of confirming has a certain unadjectivable voluptuousness.

Las palabras hubieran podido salvarme, pero estoy demasiado viviente. No, no quiero cantar muerte. Mi muerte ... el lobo gris ... la matadora que viene de la lejanía ... ¿No hay un alma viva en esta ciudad? Porque ustedes están muertos. ¿Y qué espera puede convertirse en esperanza si están todos muertos? ¿Y cuándo vendrá lo que esperamos? ¿Cuándo dejaremos de huir? ¿Cuándo ocurrirá todo esto? ¿Cuándo? ¿Dónde? ¿Cómo? ¿Cuánto? ¿Por qué? ¿Para quién?

Words would've been able to save me, only I'm much too alive. No, I don't want to sing of death. My death ... the grey wolf ... the huntress who closes in from a distance ... Is there no living soul left in this city? Because all of you are dead. And how will expecting ever turn into expectation if everyone is dead? And this thing we're waiting for, when will it arrive? When will we stop running away? When will all of this happen? When? Where? How? How much? Why? For whom?

NOTES AND ACKNOWLEDGMENTS

These translations are based on the original Spanish texts as they appear in Alejandra Pizarnik, *Poesía completa*, edited and compiled by Ana Becciù (Barcelona: Editorial Lumen, 2000). The preface by Julio Cortázar is excerpted from a letter to Alejandra Pizarnik, dated July 14, 1965, included in the compiled *Cartas* (Madrid: Alfaguara, 2012). Translated here by Yvette Siegert.

Page 13: "Cold in Hand Blues" is a song written by Jack Gee and Fred Longshaw in 1925. That same year, Columbia Records released an album with a performance of the song that featured Longshaw, Bessie Smith, and Louis Armstrong.

Pages 23 and 29: *The Garden of Earthly Delights*, housed at the Museo del Prado, in Madrid, is a triptych painted by the Dutch master Hieronymus Bosch (1450–1516) sometime between 1490 and 1510. The title poem of the collection refers to the "hell" panel, which depicts musicians playing on garish instruments that are used for torture.

Page 35: *Les Chants de Maldoror* is a long narrative prose poem by the Comte de Lautréamont, the pseudonym of the precocious Uruguayan-born French Surrealist writer Isidore Lucien Ducasse (1846–1870). Lautréamont's work played a significant role in the Surrealist movement and, as a result, was highly influential in Pizarnik's imagery and use of prose forms.

Page 45: The line "L'obscurité des eaux" is from *Le Téâtre et son double*, a collection of essays by the French writer, actor, and theater director Antonin Artaud (1896–1948). The original text reads: *Mais d'une autre realité dangereuse et typique, ou les Principes, comme les dauphins, quand ils ont montré leur tête s'empressent de rentrer dans l'obscurité des eaux.*

Parts of this manuscript were presented at the first international congress on the works of Alejandra Pizarnik, organized by Adéla-ïde de Chatellus and Milagros Ezquerro at the Université de Paris-Sorbonne (Paris IV), in November 2012. The poem "Cornerstone" first appeared, in a slightly different version, in *Guernica: A Journal of Literature and Art*, in April 2013.

The translator would like to thank Jeffrey Yang, Barbara Epler, and the staff of New Directions. Sincere gratitude to Ana Becciù and Myriam Pizarnik de Nesis, as well as to Sylvia Molloy, Madeleine Stratford, and Michael Scammell for their careful reading of these translations. Minú Prom Croche provided elegant copyediting assistance with the Spanish text, and Tayt Harlin offered invaluable editorial advice along the way. For their sensibility and encouragement, heartfelt thanks to Isabel Cadenas Cañón, Theodora Danylevich, Étienne Dobenesque, Jessica Feldman, David Francis, David Gerrard, Edith Grossman, Ricardo Maldonado, Águeda Rayo, Diana Reese, Jennifer Stahl, Erica Wright, Daniel Zalewski, and Alan Ziegler. This project could not have been completed without the loving patience of family, especially Lucas Alvarez, Elkin Ochoa Siegert, Vera Parma Siegert, Minú Prom Croche, and Jorge Pabello Olmos.